An Introduction to Coping with

Extreme Emotions

D1081742

An Introduction to Coping with
Extreme Emotions

Dr Lee Brosan
and
Dr Amanda Spong

ROBINSON

ROBINSON

First published in Great Britain in 2017 by Robinson

3 5 7 9 10 8 6 4 2

Copyright © Lee Brosan and Amanda Spong, 2017

p. 109: Taken from *Mindfulness: A Practical Guide to Finding Peace in a Frantic World* by Mark Williams and Dr Danny Penman

The moral rights of the authors have been asserted.

A CIP catalogue record for this book
is available from the British Library.

Important note
This book is not intended as a substitute for medical advice or treatment. Any person with a condition requiring medical attention should consult a qualified medical practitioner or suitable therapist.

ISBN: 978-1-47213-732-6

Typeset in Bembo by Initial Typesetting Services, Edinburgh
Printed and bound by Clays Ltd, Elcograf S.p.A.

Papers used by Robinson are from well-managed forests
and other responsible sources.

MIX
Paper from
responsible sources
FSC® C104740

Robinson
An imprint of
Little, Brown Book Group
Carmelite House
50 Victoria Embankment
London EC4Y 0DZ

An Hachette UK Company
www.hachette.co.uk
www.littlebrown.co.uk

Contents

Contents

Some things to consider before reading this book

After we had written this book, we showed it to some service users who had a diagnosis of personality disorder. They gave us really useful feedback, which we have used to improve the book. They also suggested it would be helpful to have a page at the start about how to use the book – so here it is! We would like to thank them for their time and help. We would also like to thank Dr Alice Liddell (clinical psychologist) and Lucy Fergusson (assistant psychologist) for their time supporting service users to give their feedback and reporting the results of these focus groups. Lastly, we would like to thank Lynn Eldred (community psychiatric nurse) for her contribution to the section on mindfulness.

We started writing this book when we realised that quite a few of the people we worked with had been given a diagnosis of personality disorder – usually

Borderline Personality Disorder (BPD) – but didn't have a very clear idea of what this meant. We started to run psycho-educational groups, but were aware that some people did not want to discuss their problems in a group. Sadly, not everyone has the opportunity to have someone sit with them individually to go over the diagnosis and help them think about what it means to them. We also hoped that people might be able to show the book to their family and friends to help them to understand the diagnosis a little better. This might be particularly true of the section on self-harm.

Our next strategy, then, was to write something that people could take away with them and discuss with a key worker, care co-ordinator, close friend or family member. Our hope was that it would be helpful if there was a single document that could be shared with the person who had been diagnosed with BPD and enable them to understand what the diagnosis meant to them, how it related to their difficulties, and what they could do to adjust their lifestyle and coping strategies to minimise the disruption BPD might be causing in their lives.

How to use this book

The best way that we think the book can be used is *that it should be read in small sections – and no more than one chapter at a time*. If you want to split the introduction in half, then stop after the section on understanding extreme emotions. Then give yourself time for what you've read to sink in. It can be helpful to keep notes so that you start to notice when you might be doing or thinking things that are described in the book. Often the book suggests exercises for you to carry out, and you will get more from it if you go along with these. One exercise is to write a crisis plan for yourself that you would be able to use. Hopefully by that stage you will have had time to become clear what to do and to practise some of the strategies involved.

Some service users said that reading through the book was a bit overwhelming and made them feel that it was too much to take in. Others found that the sections on self-harm and attachment sometimes triggered difficult memories or emotions, although this was not the case for everyone; bear this in mind before you start reading those sections. So we'd just like to say that before you go through the whole book, make sure that you are somewhere safe, or that you have thought of someone you can call to talk to about how you feel after reading, if you need to.

As we said, *we would recommend having someone who can support you when you are reading the book, a person you trust to be able to listen to you.* We think this is important and that people should not be given this book to read alone. So before you start reading, identify someone – or more than one person – you would feel comfortable sharing the book with, someone you can contact if you feel you need to talk through what it has brought up for you, or who would be able to go through it with you.

Lastly, if you can identify someone like this, it might be particularly helpful to share your crisis plan and the section on self-harm with them. If you want to share more, and they are interested, then of course do so!

Part 1: UNDERSTANDING EMOTIONS AND BORDERLINE PERSONALITY DISORDER

Introduction

Almost everyone will have experienced emotions. We all feel happy when things are going our way and sad or cross when they're not. Most of us feel frightened if we think something bad is going to happen to us, and feel sympathy if we hear about bad things happening to other people. Most of us will experience quite extreme emotions at some point in our lives, too. We'll have felt rage if we think we've been treated unfairly, and terrible sadness if someone close to us has died. We might have found it very difficult to cope with how we feel.

We also know that emotions vary greatly between people. Some people experience emotions much more strongly than others, and find them much harder to cope with. Sometimes the problems of experiencing emotions can become overwhelming, so that people really struggle with how they feel. They may do all sorts of things to avoid emotion, or to try to get rid of emotions when they occur. They might find themselves doing very destructive things as a result of not being able to stand how they feel.

People who have a diagnosis of Borderline Personality Disorder (BPD) will almost all struggle with their emotions. We now know that emotions are one of the core problems of this disorder. In fact, extreme emotions are so typical of BPD that there is a move to call it Emotionally Unstable Personality Disorder instead.

In this book we are going to explain what Borderline Personality Disorder is, and how it may affect you. Sometimes people have some features of BPD without having the actual diagnosis, but still really struggle with their emotions.

The book will focus on how to understand, recognise and manage your emotions. It will explain how having traits of or a diagnosis of Borderline Personality Disorder can make these skills more difficult to develop. Finally it will give some practical advice about how paying attention to your routines and lifestyle choices can enhance the emotional skills you have learned in this book. We do not, however, have the space to address the impact that emotional difficulties and Borderline Personality Disorder can have on your relationships with other people. If this is an important area to you, and one that you are looking to address, we make some recommendations in the appendix about where you can get information and support.

2

Understanding emotions

So what are emotions all about? There are two important facts about emotions: first that emotions are useful, and second that they have evolved over a long period of time and that this has implications for how they work.

A note on words for emotions: In this book we use the words 'feeling' and 'emotion' interchangeably. Some people argue that the words have slightly different meanings, but we won't be going into the difference here. And we use the word 'distress' to mean any sort of feeling that is unpleasant and causes problems for the person who experiences it.

Emotions are useful

Because emotions can be so horrible to experience, we might ask why we have them. What is the point? Scientists have argued about this a lot, but the common idea is that:

Emotions are useful to us, and help us to survive.

It can be very difficult for us to believe this, especially if we have problems with emotions, either our own or other people's. But, if we take three examples, we can start to see how useful emotions can be.

Anger

Anger can be very difficult and frightening. Many people with emotional problems have been on the receiving end of anger and know how terrifying it often is, and how unjust it can feel to be the recipient of it. Sometimes people are frightened of their own anger, too, and would do anything to avoid it. What could be good about it?

In fact, people say that anger spurs them on to do something about things that they think are wrong – stepping in when they see bullying, for example, or campaigning for civil rights. It can help people to stand up for themselves when they need to. Sometimes when people get angry with themselves it can help make them determined not to act like that again.

Fear

Fear has a very useful function for us. Imagine ourselves as early man living on the savannah with lions and other dangerous animals. If we weren't frightened when we saw them, then we wouldn't take action to avoid them, and that would be the end of us! Many people will have heard of the 'fight-or-flight' response which occurs when we are frightened. Fear stimulates our bodies to become highly efficient at coping with physical danger by fighting or running away. It's true that a lot of situations that make us frightened nowadays don't require a physical response, but that's a story for another time. The point here is that fear can be really helpful to us.

Sadness

Sadness is a bit more of a puzzle, but one way to think about it is that we become sad, very often, when we have lost something precious to us. Maybe sadness reminds us to stay close to people or things that are important, and take better care of them. Some people also think that sadness might be a message to you that things aren't right in your world, so that you can start to put them right. It might also work by sending a message to other people that we need to be cared for.

Emotion as communication

Another way in which emotion can be useful is that it communicates to other people how we feel. If we think about emotion, particularly extreme emotion, we can see that it changes the way we look and the way we sound. Look at the previous pictures – they are caricatures, but they do show how different we look when we are in a particular emotional state. The sad person is stooped and bent – their body has no energy; if we heard them talking, their voice would probably be quiet and slow. On the other hand, the angry person exudes energy, and their posture is likely to be very upright, making them appear larger than normal; their voice is likely to be loud and they will probably talk fast.

All this sends messages to other people that allow them to adapt their behaviour accordingly. So, if you see someone who is sad, you might ask them what the matter is – you might feel sympathy and try to help them. By communicating sadness, the sad person thus attracts the care and support from others that they need. And if you see someone who is angry, you might well avoid them – so you get yourself out of danger, just in case they decide they're angry at you! Communicating emotions means that people can share feelings, and can form emotional bonds with other people. Remember that we are social animals – most people are happier with others than alone – and that the communication and sharing of emotion is a very good way of strengthening our social bonds. We look after each other, we understand things from other people's perspective; we learn that something we've done is not acceptable to others.

'I'm so happy, I love everyone.'

Of course, we don't always want to communicate our emotions – anyone who has played poker can vouch for that – so we can also learn to hide our emotions from others when we need to. Some people call this their 'mask'. We might hide our emotions when we have decided that it is not in our interests to show them, or because our past experiences have taught us that some emotions lead to dangerous or frightening reactions from other people.

The evolution of emotion

Many thousands of years ago, humans lived in woods, or on the open savannah, in social groups, or tribes. The tribe had to survive among many other animals, some much stronger and bigger than us. We saw in the previous section how useful it was for us to feel fear in threatening situations, and how useful to have the 'fight-or-flight' response in which adrenaline is released and our bodies become stronger and faster. There are also other responses to fear, such as 'freezing', where you go very still and motionless. This has obvious survival value when you consider that many predators' vision is based on movement – it's much harder to see something when it's still. Anyone who has seen the film *Jurassic Park* will know all about that! Sometimes we still freeze now – people talk about being paralysed by fear.

There were also other aspects of emotion that developed in our social groups. Most humans couldn't survive on their own, so it was important for members of a group to like each other if they were going to stay together. So humans developed emotions of liking and love that helped the group to bond.

'Emotion brain' and 'thinking brain'

Because our emotions developed so early in our evolution, they are controlled by an old part of our brain called the limbic system – the 'emotion brain'. This part of our brain doesn't just control emotions relating to danger, but all our other emotions, too – love, hate, anger, sadness. The fact that our emotions are controlled by this old part of our brain means that they are very quick and automatic – we don't think much when emotion is triggered, we just feel and react quickly.

As humans developed, our brains became more sophisticated, and a newer part developed – the 'thinking brain' – which allows us to think and analyse situations. This part of the brain allows us to weigh up the pros and cons of what we might do, and keeps the emotion brain under control so that we can plan what we want to do, and work out what's best for us. For instance, if we saw the leader of the troop munching on a steak, we might feel hunger and want to snatch it out of his hands, but the newly developing thinking brain might say: 'Er, no, probably better not to, or he'll rip my head off.' The thinking brain overrides the emotion brain, so that although we still feel hunger, we are able to suppress the desire to act on it, and can learn to manage how we feel.

However, in some situations, our old emotion brain still takes over, and shuts down the thinking brain. This happens when we are in situations where we need to respond quickly, or when our emotions are very strong. If you are faced with a double-decker bus coming down the middle of the road towards you, it's not very sensible to stand there thinking, 'Hmm, I wonder if the driver can see me, or if he'll have time to put the brakes on and stop before he gets to me'! You need to get out of the way fast – and it's our emotion brains that control this reaction.

Obviously this is a good idea in situations like avoiding a bus, but the problem is that our thinking brains can go offline in *any* situation when we feel strong emotions. So we stop thinking and considering the consequences, and just react. If you are having an argument with your partner, for instance, and he or she says something you don't like, it's highly likely that your emotions will be very quickly triggered and you'll respond by saying something worse. So the emotion brain takes over and the argument escalates, even though that might not be what either of you really wanted. Another example is dealing with bureaucracy – it's really easy to get taken over by the emotion brain, and end up saying or doing things which don't exactly smooth the process. Thumping the traffic warden really isn't going to help.

So the old emotion brain has advantages and disadvantages. It can protect us from danger, but it can also lead us to do things that probably aren't the most sensible way to solve the problem!

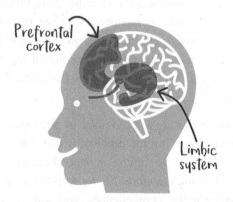

Fig. 1: The limbic system and prefrontal cortex

The development of the 'thinking brain'

Like the emotion brain, our new 'thinking brain' has advantages and disadvantages. It enables us to carry out much more sophisticated processes, such as self-reflection and self-monitoring – that is, we're able to think about what we're doing, and to stop our automatic responses. This helps us to function in a more sophisticated way with each other and our surroundings, which is especially helpful now that the situations that we find ourselves in are often very complex. Sadly, however, our new thinking brain also has a downside.

The downside of the 'thinking brain'

The downside is that we have started to be able to think about ourselves, and to weigh ourselves up, just as we weigh up other people and situations around us. We think about what sort of people we are, what other people think of us, how we fit into a situation. Sadly this means that we have become capable of self-doubt and self-criticism.

For instance, say that you have agreed to go bungee jumping with friends. As you get to the top of the jump, you might feel absolute terror and think, 'There is no way on Earth that I'm jumping off this.' But the thinking brain says, 'Yeah, but if you don't, your mates are going to think you're an absolute wimp.' So the terror of the emotion brain, and the more sophisticated fear of rejection of the thinking brain, are in conflict. Do you jump?

'Oh no, my emotion brain's in charge!'

The interaction between the old brain and the new brain can go very wrong, but it can also help us. Take Nicky, who had a family wedding coming up, but knew that her cousin, who had bullied her very badly when she was little, would be there. She really wanted to avoid going, and was terrified about what would happen. What she was afraid of could be described as in Figure 2.

Fig. 2 When the interaction between old brain and new brain goes wrong

Trigger: Seeing my cousin at the wedding

Old brain emotion: Fear that he'll bully and humiliate me

Fear worsens

New brain thinking:

He knows I'm still scared; he'll go for me

He'll be able to see how frightened of him I am

Behaviour:

Stammer, go red, can't speak

Fig. 3 When the interaction between the old brain and the new brain goes right

Trigger: Seeing my cousin at the wedding

Old brain emotion: Fear that he'll bully and intimidate me

New brain thinking:
I'm smart and funny and if he starts anything I'm going to get him!

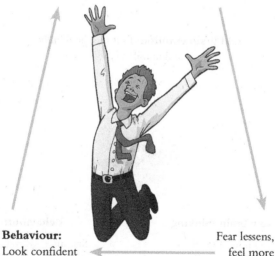

Behaviour:
Look confident talk to loads of people.

Say hello briefly to the bully, who looks quite embarrassed himself

Fear lessens, feel more confident

Using the thinking brain better

Even though Nicky was really scared that her cousin might bully and humiliate her at the wedding, she tried to get her 'thinking brain' to work a bit better, as shown in Figure 3. She said to herself, 'I know he used to bully me, and hurt me, too, but that was a long time ago. I'm not a little girl now, and actually I'm quite smart and funny, so if he starts anything I can easily defend myself. And anyway, he might even be quite ashamed of what he was like, unless he's a complete thug. And I've got loads of friends there, too.'

Summary

Emotions are normal and useful and help to protect us. As we've evolved, our thinking processes have become intricately linked with emotion so that they can both help and hinder how we manage them. You might like to note down in the box overleaf what you've learned about emotions in this chapter.

What I have learned about emotions	What problems do my emotions cause me?	What do I want to change?

3

Understanding extreme emotions

So now we understand a bit about emotions. But why is it that they are so much more extreme in some people than in others? There seem to be two answers to this: first our biological sensitivity to emotion, and second what we've learned about emotions.

Biological sensitivity

To think about this, let's go back to our group of early men and women, managing to survive in an environment full of hostile groups and dangerous animals. All of these need to be avoided or overcome when our group is trying to find food, shelter, and time to relax and bond with each other. Now imagine that everyone in the group is extremely relaxed. When there's a rustle in the undergrowth everyone says, 'No need to worry, it's just the wind.' Then the lions come out of the undergrowth and eat half the tribe.

So that won't do. To survive, the group needs members who are highly reactive, sensitive to danger and prepared to think the worst. When there's a rustle in the undergrowth the group needs people who react and yell 'Danger!' and get everyone to panic and move away. Once the group has moved somewhere else, then the calm people have a chance to say, 'It's OK, we're safe now,' and settle everyone down. So the group needs both kinds of people, and a lot in the middle, too, to keep the balance. We can't all be calm and laid back.

'Who, me? I never would!'

What this means is that within our human population there is a lot of difference in reactivity, because that's what's kept us alive. Biological reactivity, or sensitivity, became coded in our nervous system and passed on in our genes. People with extreme emotions are in some ways like the very reactive individuals in our example – much more likely to become highly aroused at triggers, to react as if there is danger, and to take a long time to settle.

So one reason why some people find it harder than others to accept their emotions is simply that their emotions are much more extreme. All the physiological aspects of emotion get fired off very quickly, are very extreme, and don't wear off immediately. A small trigger can produce severe reactions for such a person, whereas for someone else they might just create a low level of emotional arousal.

What we learn about emotions in childhood

The second reason that some people experience extreme emotions is to do with what we learn about emotions when we are young. If children have been brought up in an environment where they've been comforted if they are upset, and where adults help them to understand their feelings, then they are much more likely to be able to tolerate the emotions they later experience. On the other hand, if a child is punished for being upset, or ignored, or told to go away or 'stop crying or I'll give you something to cry about', then obviously their experience of emotions is much more frightening. This means that when those children grow up they have learned that emotions are something to be scared of. They can't accept the emotions, and can't tolerate having them.

Some talk about the 'invalidating environment', a term introduced by Marsha Linehan, who developed the psychological therapy Dialectical Behaviour Therapy (DBT). This is when you feel something but the people around you tell you that you are wrong to feel that way. They might deny that things that upset you have happened, or tell you that you're crazy. We'll talk about all this in a bit more detail in the next section, on attachment.

It seems to be this combination of biological sensitivity, and an early environment that punished and invalidated emotional experience, that is so crucially important in the development of emotional disorders. And it can make you feel like this:

Of course, we should say here that not everyone who experiences extreme emotions finds them a problem. There are people who can tolerate very strong feelings, almost value them. They might like the physical sensations of emotion, and maybe think that it means they are more alive. It seems that it's what we've learned about how we feel that really makes the difference, just as much as what we actually feel.

Conditions of early life and attachment

In the section above we spoke about the impact of early environments on our emotions, but there is more to it than that!

There are a lot of different psychological theories about human development, but nearly everyone agrees that early experiences in life play a large part in shaping our personalities. If our early experiences have been very negative then we are much more likely to develop personality problems, or personality disorders. There are certain things that children need in order to develop healthy selves, particularly what's known as 'attachment' to others, and if this process goes wrong then it too can lead to personality problems.

We are all born with the need to form emotional bonds with the adults who look after us – usually our parents, but not always. *Attachment* is the name that we give to the emotional bond between two human beings, although these bonds are observed in most mammals. Attachment is necessary for survival; its purpose is to protect vulnerable young against danger through the development of emotional bonds with those who take care of them, and the need to develop attachment is a hard-wired instinct that we all have. These bonds develop into patterns as we grow, and these patterns are shaped by the usual responses that the child gets from the parent or other caregiver.

Secure attachment develops when the parent meets the needs of the child in a fairly consistent way. For example, if the child cries because it is thirsty, the parent works this out fairly quickly and provides a drink. The parent does not have to get it right first time, or in fact all the time: what is necessary is 'good enough' care. So, if the parent gets it wrong but realises this and shows concern and puts it right, this can strengthen the attachment.

Insecure attachment happens when the caregiver consistently fails to understand and respond to the child's needs. There are two different patterns of insecure attachment.

Overinvolved attachment develops when the parent has responded to the child's needs erratically.

Sometimes they have provided what the child needs, but not often. So the child learns to exaggerate its communication in order to have its needs met. With this attachment pattern, the child may cry or protest excessively in order to get attention and have its needs met. As the caregiver responds to the child's needs some of the time, it is worth the child making repeated or exaggerated attempts to communicate.

Avoidant attachment develops when the parent fairly consistently fails to meet the needs of the child, or consistently misunderstands its needs, or offers a negative or frightening response, such as ridicule or punishment. For example, if the child says, 'I am thirsty, I need a drink,' and the parent responds, 'Don't be so stupid, you've already had a drink,' the child learns that it is safer to keep its needs to itself. Over time this suppresses the child's needs to quite an extreme degree. This means that when distressed the child may not show any emotion, although inside its heart is racing and other stress responses are working overtime.

Once we have learned these attachment patterns, we tend to see all relationships in that way, and repeat the patterns in our subsequent relationships as we grow and mature. Attachment patterns, and the strategies for getting our needs met that go along with them, are activated in stressful situations when we need safety and comfort. It is not difficult to see how either of the insecure attachment patterns could lead to difficulties in managing distress and getting support from other people when we need it. For example, does someone express high levels of anger when they are feeling vulnerable (over-involved attachment) or do they seem distanced and emotionally flat (avoidant attachment)?

It is important to say that these reactions are not 'attention seeking'. Many people with personality disorder often have this label used unkindly against them. But the behaviours described within these attachment patterns are not used consciously to elicit reactions from others. They are strategies that were developed early in life, usually as a means for emotional, or perhaps physical, survival.

However, there is good news here, too. As we grow and come into contact with a range of people, we continue to learn about emotions and develop emotional bonds. This means that, under the right circumstances, children who have developed an insecure attachment pattern with their parents can develop secure attachments with other adults, such as grandparents or teachers.

There are, of course, many ways in which an environment can be much more negative. Some people who develop personality disorders have had severely traumatic upbringings. They may have been subject to abuse of some kind. Sexual abuse is very common among people with personality disorders, but so is physical and emotional abuse – and often, of course, the three go together. Other ways in which an environment can be negative is through neglect. At the extreme end this can mean that children's most basic physical needs for food, clothes, a toilet, and a clean dry place to sleep and live are ignored. Psychological neglect is also extremely important – the carer may put his or her own needs before the child's, and expect the child to do so as well. If no one ever cares how you feel, or what you think, and even punishes you for making demands, it's easy to see that you would grow up thinking that you are not important, and not worth anything to anyone. We've already mentioned the 'invalidating environment'. With regards to children, this can mean that the child learns that its views on things are at odds with everyone else's, and that its needs are less important than other people's. Personality difficulties can also be made worse later, when the child goes to school and often around puberty. People who are being abused at home can find it very hard to fit in at school, and are often subject to bullying and abuse by others.

The interaction of biological sensitivity and early environment

As with extreme emotions, not everyone who is biologically sensitive develops a personality disorder, nor does everyone who has been badly treated in childhood, or whose attachment patterns are insecure. Again, it seems to be the case that these things add together. So if you are biologically sensitive, *and* your early environment is invalidating, with insecure attachment, then you are much more likely to develop problems. As we said earlier, it is very common for people with BPD to experience very strong emotions which they find hard to control.

Personality disorder and the emotion brain

If you have a personality disorder, it is likely that you will have experienced an early environment that made it hard for you to cope with emotions, and it's also quite likely that you are biologically more sensitive to emotion. As a result, your old emotion brain is triggered more easily, and takes longer to return to a state that enables your thinking brain to come back on line. This means that you may react more easily to triggers, perhaps in a more extreme way, and take longer to calm down again. You will therefore need to work harder and more consciously on developing strategies to help you compensate for this and minimise the damage that may ensue either for yourself or for your relationships. We hope that this book will help you to do this.

4

What is Borderline Personality Disorder?

The term Borderline Personality Disorder was coined a long time ago to describe a condition that seemed to fall between two old diagnostic categories – 'neurotic' mental health problems, which have at their core extreme forms of emotional distress, such as obsessions or depression, and 'psychotic' problems, which occur when the person experiences themselves or the world around them in profoundly different but rigid ways, perhaps believing they see or hear things that others cannot (hallucinations), or having fixed views that are thought to be irrational by others (delusions). People who have BPD can experience both strong emotions and temporary psychotic phenomena; in other words, they are on the borderline between the two.

We don't really think about mental illness in this way any more, but the term 'borderline personality disorder' has stuck. However, the term Emotionally Unstable Personality Disorder is now sometimes used because it gives a clearer description of the difficulties associated with the diagnosis.

Difficulties with emotion are one of the core problems that people with BPD experience, but there are a range of other problems that go with the disorder. We'll start by describing what these are, so that you can assess how far these symptoms apply to you.

BPD: a general description

As we've seen, most of us may experience extremes of emotion. Sometimes these extremes can be very unstable, so that the mood of a person with a personality disorder flips from one state to another with almost no warning. It can be very hard for people with BPD to cope with this instability, and occasionally they find ways of coping with their emotions that aren't helpful – by hurting themselves, or by taking it out on others. They might do things in a very impulsive way, forgetting that these impulsive acts have consequences which may well backfire. Very often people with BPD find it hard to trust others, and fear that others will reject or abandon them. This can be because people with BPD hate themselves so much that they can't imagine that anyone else could feel differently about them, or because important people in their lives, such as their parents, have treated them like this in the past (remember what we said about attachment).

Basically, we can put the symptoms into three categories:

1. problems with emotions

2. problems with behaviour

3. problems with relationships.

The symptoms are all described in the fifth edition of the *Diagnostic and Statistical Manual for Mental Disorders*, usually known as DSM. This is the major system of classifying mental disorders used by professionals. In order to be given a diagnosis of BPD you need to have six or more of these symptoms, but if you have fewer you might still be experiencing quite a lot of problems with the ones you do have! Doctors or health professionals might say that you have mild BPD or traits of BPD.

Symptoms of BPD

1 Problems with emotions

Affective instability

In mental health services, emotion is sometimes referred to as affect, so affective instability refers to problems with your emotions. As you will know, your emotions can fluctuate extremely rapidly and very violently, sometimes flipping from one state to another with no warning. You might wake up some days in an extreme mood, while at other times you will be in one mood for a few hours and then almost out of the blue your mood can change drastically. You might go from feeling OK to feeling furiously angry or upset, or extremely depressed. You might have somewhat 'high' moods, when you feel keyed up and energetic, and moods where you can hardly raise your head off the pillow because you feel so low. You might have times of extreme anxiety.

Make a note here of anything you experience that fits this description:

_____

_____

_____

_____

_____

_____

Chronic feelings of emptiness

People have described this as having a huge void that needs to be filled, or feeling that something vital to existence is missing. It could feel as if you are nothing and nobody. It might be a terrible and overwhelming sense of boredom. These feelings can sometimes prompt you to self-harm in order to try to feel something, or may cause you to do something else impulsive and probably harmful.

Again, make a note below of anything you experience that fits this description:

_____

_____

_____

_____

_____

_____

Feelings of intense anger

These can occur seemingly at any time, often out of the blue. You may feel overwhelmed with intense anger, or find it extremely difficult to control your anger. You may have frequent outbursts of temper, lash out at other people, or smash things around you. Sometimes people can get into a lot of physical fights. Sometimes the anger can be triggered by something very small (in the grand scale of things), like someone pulling out in front of you in the road, or edging in front of you in a queue.

Make a note here of anything you experience that fits this description:

_____

_____

Paranoid ideas and 'dissociative' symptoms

At times you might feel so bad that your mind almost plays tricks on you. You might start to think that people are talking about you, laughing at you or threatening you. You might think that people are plotting against you. Sometimes you might be able to tell that it's not really happening, but at other times the thoughts become so overwhelming that you really believe that it is. Another 'trick' that your mind can play is to put you into a state where you are completely cut off from what is going on around you – you become completely dissociated from your surroundings, and can't relate to what is going on around you at all. It might appear to others as if you are in a kind of trance. Sometimes the dissociation can be so extreme that you become almost like another person – this is particularly true if you have been badly abused and hurt as a child.

Make a note here of anything you experience that fits this description:

_____

_____

_____

_____

_____

_____

_____

2 Problems with behaviour

Impulsivity

People with BPD can behave very impulsively, and often in self-damaging ways. You might spend a lot of money that you can't afford, or have sex with people impulsively and dangerously. Sometimes this sexual behaviour can put you in a lot of danger. You may put yourself in other risky situations, such as driving recklessly, and otherwise taking chances with your life. You might binge eat and find it very hard to control your eating. You might drink far too much, or use other substances that might do you harm. You might not do these things with the deliberate intent to harm yourself, but nevertheless the behaviours can be highly damaging.

Make a note here of anything you experience that fits this description:

_____

_____

_____

_____

_____

_____

Suicidal behaviour and self-harm

This is a much more conscious and deliberate form of self-harm than that described above. You might hurt yourself by cutting or burning yourself. You may mutilate yourself in quite serious ways. You may take overdoses, sometimes with the intention of killing yourself, but sometimes simply to try to get some respite. Occasionally you'll do these things secretively, but at other times you'll tell other people what you are planning, maybe because you are desperate for them to understand how bad you feel.

Make a note here of anything you experience that fits this description:

_____

_____

_____

_____

_____

_____

_____

3 problems with relationships

Fear of abandonment

You might be very frightened that people are going to reject and abandon you. Sometimes the fear is so great that you think people are abandoning you even when they're not. Frequently, people go to great lengths to avoid being abandoned, perhaps by clinging on to others, demanding reassurance, or threatening to hurt themselves. Although this behaviour is very understandable, it can have very negative consequences, pushing others away so that your fear of abandonment might come true. Alternatively, you might find that you can sometimes deliberately be horrible, so that you push people away and almost force them to reject you.

People say that it's easier when the situation is under your control.

Make a note here of anything you experience that fits this description:

_____

_____

_____

_____

_____

Unstable relationships

Relationship Status:
it's complicated

Your relationships can be very intense, with extremes of good and bad feelings. Sometimes you might switch very rapidly from good to bad, especially if you think the other person has let you down, or abandoned you. This pattern happens both with your intimate relationships and with friends, and sometimes with staff who might be trying to help you. You might find that you either like people a lot or dislike them a lot, with not much in the middle. You might put people on a pedestal, and then want to knock them off when they don't live up to your hopes and expectations.

Make a note here of anything you experience that
fits this description:

_____

_____

_____

_____

_____

Identity disturbance

This means that you have a very insecure and unstable self-image, or view of yourself. We've put this
symptom in the relationship category because your
sense of yourself has such a profound effect on your
relationships with other people. You might find

it very hard to know or understand yourself, and might change dramatically according to who you are with, without having much sense of what is the 'real you'. It might be hard for you to know what you want, or what you like, or even what your true feelings are. You might have a very strong sense that you are bad or 'disgusting' and that sooner or later other people will cotton on to this.

Make a note here of anything you experience that fits this description:

_____

_____

_____

_____

_____

_____

Summary of your symptoms

Now that you have been through the descriptions, have a look at the following list and tick each symptom that you have noted applies to you, so that you and the people working with you can see it at a glance. As we have noted, people with BPD will tend to have at least six symptoms to a significant degree, although these may be experienced with different intensity at different times.

Affective instability	☐
Chronic feelings of emptiness	☐
Feelings of intense anger	☐
Paranoid ideas and 'dissociative' symptoms	☐
	☐
Impulsivity	☐
Suicidal behaviour and self-harm	☐
Fear of abandonment	☐
Unstable relationships	☐
Identity disturbance	☐
Total number of symptoms experienced	☐

5

What is a personality disorder?

Up until now we've talked specifically about BPD, but we thought that it might be helpful here to say a bit in general about personality disorders. We all have personalities – we all have different traits, or characteristics. We like to dress a certain way, associate with a certain kind of person; we might tend to be bossy, or kind, or calm, or excitable. Furthermore, almost all of us have parts of our personality that cause us problems. Many of us might sometimes get angry quickly, or get fed up with other people, or be changeable in our moods. So what is the difference between these personality difficulties and a personality disorder? The best way to think of it is by the 'three Ps' – problematic, persistent, and pervasive.

Problematic means that the characteristics cause problems for you. They make it difficult for you to get on with other people or to function very well in the world. They might make you unhappy, or cause unhappiness to other people.

Persistent means that the problem goes on over long periods of time. It's not that you have a phase of your life when you feel unsettled or moody, but that you are like that most of the time. You might have started to feel like this in adolescence or early adulthood and continued to do so throughout your life.

Pervasive means that the problems affect almost all areas of your life. It's not that you have had one difficult and stormy relationship, but that all your relationships run into the same kind of difficulties, whether they're at work, at home or in the pub. You might feel the same regardless of where you are and what's happening.

Put together, the three Ps can help to explain the difference between normal personality difficulties and personality disorder. What's important, though, is that it's not an 'either/or' situation – that you have either a 'normal' personality or a personality disorder. It's helpful to think of personality difficulties as lying on a continuum. Some lucky people have very few problematic characteristics; others might tend to have some but be able to control them in most circumstances; some might behave in ways that alienate others and make themselves unhappy, although the problems wouldn't be severe enough to be diagnosed as a 'disorder'. Personality disorders are at the far end of this continuum, but even within the category of personality disorders there are quite large differences in severity, and in the kinds of problems that people experience. The three vignettes that follow will give you some idea of these differences. So it's not that you're completely different from other people, although it undoubtedly feels like that – you're like them, but more so!

Mild: Vicky

Vicky found it fairly easy to make friends at school. She was teased for her ginger hair but her parents thought she managed this just fine. In adolescence, she became sensitive to comments about her appearance and had low self-esteem, although she remained popular and worked hard to show she could 'make something of herself'. She now holds down a busy job in a finance department but becomes quickly overwhelmed if her bosses put too much pressure on her or she misses deadlines. She can suffer with stomach problems and headaches and needs to take time off work when this happens.

Moderate: Martin

Martin's mother had depression on and off during his childhood. His father worked long hours and so he learned to take care of himself. At school, his teachers were concerned that he seemed distracted and found it hard to concentrate. Although he was very capable, he started to fall behind, particularly as his GCSEs approached. He became increasingly disruptive in class and got into some fights when he was teased for being 'stupid'. When he started to binge drink at sixteen, his anger became highly problematic. He would fly into rages if he felt 'disrespected'. He is now in a steady relationship with Sue, but finds his anger unpredictable and embarrassing. He has stopped going out in case he loses his cool again and Sue leaves him.

Severe: Joanne

Joanne's parents used to fight a lot. Her dad could be violent towards her mother and Joanne sometimes witnessed this. When she was twelve, her mother left with Joanne and they moved away. Joanne felt isolated and found it hard to make friends. At school, she would easily become angry when teachers reprimanded her and she was often in detention. At home, she isolated herself and found her mother difficult to talk to. She started dating Dan, whom she 'adored'. Dan was older than her, and had left school and got into drugs. Joanne started using speed and cocaine on a regular basis and was eventually excluded from school for her verbal and physical aggression. Her only peer network were the people she took drugs with, as she drove everyone else away. Dan could himself be volatile and Joanne was often scared of him, so she tried hard to keep him happy. She started to cut her arms and legs to shut off her fear and anger, and began to get out of it on drugs deliberately. Joanne knew this upset Dan and her family, and felt ashamed of being out of control, but when feeling overwhelmed at the time she found it impossible not to cut. Joanne often needed stitches after cutting. A&E staff tried to talk to her about her drug use and her relationship with Dan, but Joanne felt got at and would start shouting and swearing at staff.

The three Ps also apply to the difference between suffering from extreme emotions and having BPD. You might have difficulties with emotion, but they are not quite so problematic, persistent or pervasive as they would be with someone who does have that diagnosis. Whichever is the case with you, we hope that the strategies that we describe in Part 2 will help you to manage how you feel.

What about other personality disorders?

Borderline Personality Disorder is just one of a range of personality disorders, all of which require understanding and help. It seems, though, that BPD is by far the most common of these disorders, and it is the one which has been studied the most. Only Antisocial Personality Disorder has been studied to a similar extent, and has guidance from the National Institute for Health and Care Excellence (NICE) on how it can be managed. So although we know that there are different forms of personality disorder, we are concentrating on BPD, partly because it is the most common, and partly because we have some idea of how to understand and help people cope with it.

Personality disorder and stigma

We cannot deny that there has been a huge amount of stigma around the diagnosis of personality disorder, and this is true among professionals as well as the general public. The label of personality disorder had a ring of judgement and criticism to it, rather than being just a description. People with personality disorders have been seen as 'manipulative' and 'difficult'. Individuals have reported experiences in some health and social care contexts in which professionals have been hostile, or not taken their concerns seriously.

What's more, for a long time personality disorder was thought of as untreatable, and until 2007 no provision was made in the Mental Health Act for dealing with it, possibly because it was less successfully treated by medication than other disorders. This meant that people with personality disorder were excluded or marginalised by mental health services.

Thankfully, a lot of this has now changed. Mental health professionals have started to take the condition much more seriously, and to understand it better. We understand that people can be helped to change, and that the disorder can be managed differently. This understanding is also slowly filtering through to the general public. So we hope very much that the stigma will abate, and that people will get the help that they need.

What have I learned about Borderline Personality Disorder and extreme emotions?

Before we move on to the next section, it might help you to jot down a few ideas from the chapters above that you've found helpful. This doesn't have to be a complete summary of everything we've talked about, but simply ideas that it might help you to keep in mind. Other people we've talked to have said things like this:

> 'It feels like such a relief to know that there's a reason why I've always felt like this. I know I had a hard childhood, but I never realised the impact it had had on me – I thought it was just normal to be treated like that.'

> 'I love the idea that my emotions are so extreme because they helped early man to survive! When people get impatient with me I just tell myself they wouldn't even be alive if it weren't for people like me, so nah to them!'

Ideas about extreme emotions that I can keep in mind:

_____

_____

_____

_____

_____

_____

_____

_____

_____

_____

_____

_____

_____

_____

Part 2: COPING WITH EXTREME EMOTIONS AND BORDERLINE PERSONALITY DISORDER

6

Coping with crises and self-harm

Why are crises hard to manage for people with Borderline Personality Disorder and extreme emotions?

Crises happen to everybody at some point or other. Common kinds of crisis might include:

- relationship break-ups

- falling out with a friend

- changes to your benefits

- losing a job.

Such events would be difficult for anyone to deal with, but the more extreme your emotions are, the harder it will be. You will have much stronger and more intense emotional reactions, and the emotion will take much longer to die down again. Difficult events can therefore be much harder to cope with if you have BPD.

In Part 1 of this book we explained about the 'emotion' brain and the 'thinking' brain. In case you haven't read that chapter, then, very briefly, our emotion brain developed early (in evolutionary terms). Our emotion brain helps us respond quickly to external circumstances like threat. It determines what our bodies do (run away, fight, freeze) without us having to think about it, and it changes our physiology so that we can do what we need to – such as becoming very still to avoid being noticed. Because our emotion brain reacts without thinking, it can sometimes land us in quite a lot of trouble – for example, if we hit someone who has criticised us.

Our thinking brains developed much later in our evolution. The thinking brain helps us to control and manage our emotions; it weighs up situations and decides what the most sensible course of action is. It can stop the impulsive responses of the emotion brain. The problem for people who experience extreme emotions is that the emotion brain tends to be in charge a lot of the time and the thinking brain doesn't get much of a look-in.

So the more extreme your emotions, the more easily your emotion brain takes over and shuts down your ability to think about what is going on. You can't properly weigh up what's happening, or try to solve the problems that are causing the upset, or work out what is the best thing to do. So you are much more likely to react in ways that aren't helpful. Here's an example.

Molly is a young woman who really struggles with her emotions. She doesn't have many friends and is worried that people don't like her. Molly started a new job a while ago and got on well with one of her colleagues, Trish. They agreed to meet to go to the cinema, but just as she got there Molly received a text from Trish to say that she couldn't make it because of a family emergency. Molly 'knew' this was just an excuse and that Trish couldn't be bothered with her; she became wild with rage and disappointment. She rang Trish and shouted down the phone, yelling that she was an untrustworthy, selfish cow and only ever thought about herself.

Molly went home and drank a bottle of wine, and then cut herself badly with a kitchen knife to try to put all the pain behind her. She had to go to A&E because the cut was so deep. She called in sick the next day, but when she went back to work the following week she found that Trish's brother had been arrested that night, and that Trish had been called by the police to go and bail him out. Needless to say, Trish didn't want to talk to her, and the budding friendship never recovered.

In this example, it's easy to see that Molly was completely overwhelmed by her emotional brain, and that the consequences were quite harsh. She needed to go to A&E, and she spoiled a potential friendship beyond repair. Perhaps if she'd been able to stop for a short while and get her thinking brain back on line she could have asked Trish if she was OK, or if she needed help. She could have told herself that, although she was disappointed, the emergency might be genuine, and that she could at least wait to find out.

Crises and self-harm

Self-harm is a very common reaction to extreme emotion, particularly at times of crisis.

Some common types of self-harm include:

- cutting

- burning

- misusing alcohol or drugs

- taking overdoses of medication

- over- or under-eating

- engaging in risky behaviours, such as meeting up and having sex with someone you have recently met on-line. (This is something that many young people have done. You may not view it as self-harm, but it may have the same function as the other items in the list. Is it done to punish yourself or switch off unbearable emotions? If this is the case, it may be a form of self-harm.)

Self-harm is different from suicidal behaviour, because on the whole, when you self-harm you don't intend to kill yourself. In fact, some people say that self-harming actually prevents them from committing suicide, because it somehow releases pressure. Even if you don't mean to kill yourself, self-harming can be very dangerous. You might take so many overdoses of medication that your liver is affected and you become ill. Or you might get used to the amount of harm you do, and end up doing more and more so that you harm yourself beyond repair. You might need to cut deeper to feel the same level of release of emotional distress. Sometimes people can be disfigured, and can be very ashamed and need to hide themselves from others.

Despite how damaging self-harm is, it's very important to acknowledge that there are many things about it that can feel very helpful, at least in the moment that you do it:

- Physical pain can distract you from your emotional pain, or stop it altogether.

- It can give you a sense of control – at least there's something you can do.

- It can help you to feel a bit more real if you are losing any sense of yourself.

- It can help if it gets people to show that they're concerned.

It may be useful to think about all the different ways that you self-harm and to understand how it helps you. Try to fill out the form opposite every time you harm yourself. In the first column, write down what was going on before you got the urge to self-harm. Had you felt lonely? In conflict with other people? Had you spoken to someone who always winds you up? In the second column, write down what you did – cut yourself, burned yourself, took too many pills . . . Then, in the third column, write down how it helped. Did it stop you hurting psychologically? Help you to feel numb?

What was going on just before I harmed myself?	What I did to self-harm	How did it help me?

The impact of self-harm on other people

It is common for people to hide their self-harm and to feel ashamed and disgusted with themselves after they have done it. However, some self-harming behaviours are difficult to keep from people who are close to you, and at times you will need to go to A&E for help or treatment. It is inevitable that at some point your self-harming behaviours will come to the attention of your friends, family or health professionals. Self-harm often evokes an emotional reaction in others, because they find it frightening and hard to understand. It can make them feel terribly worried about you, but completely unable to help. So it can cause long-term damage to your close relationships. Even some professionals find it hard to cope with, particularly if they are trying to help you stop self-harming.

For each of the self-harming behaviours you have listed in the previous box, think about what the consequences are for your friends, family and health professionals, and how they might react. Write them in the box opposite.

Self-harm behaviour 1	Staff	
	Family	
	Friends	

Self-harm behaviour 2	Staff								
	Family								
	Friends								

When you've filled the forms out a few times, have a look and see if you can spot any patterns. How do other people react when you self-harm? What impact does it seem to have on your relationships with other people?

You may now start to have a clearer idea about why you respond the way you do in a crisis, and about the consequences of some of these behaviours. The next chapter will help you think about developing alternative and less harmful ways to cope with crises and the overwhelming emotions that can result from them. First, though, you need to be clear in your mind why you want to change your behaviours. Change can be difficult and will require you to persevere, and it will help to start with a clear rationale, one which is written down, as to why you are doing this. You can write it overleaf, but you may need to keep it somewhere you can find it whenever you have the urge to self-harm again.

Alternatives to self-harm

In the next chapter, on distress tolerance, we look at how you can think about developing more adaptive ways of coping as a replacement to self-harm for managing distress.

The reasons I self-harm are:

_____

_____

_____

_____

**The negative effects for me, my friends,
family or staff are:**

_____

_____

_____

_____

The reasons I want to stop self-harming are:

_____

_____

_____

_____

7

Distress tolerance

Do you struggle to face your feelings?

As we saw in Part 1, almost all of us have experienced very distressing feelings at some point in our lives, and probably found it very difficult to cope with how we feel. For people with BPD or other emotional problems, these extremes of emotion can be everyday occurrences, and can be unbearable to live with.

Sometimes you might not even be aware that you are struggling with feelings, so have a look at the statements below and see if you agree with any of them. If you do, put a tick in the box next to the statements you agree with.

Feeling distressed or upset is
unbearable to me ☐

When I'm upset all I can think
about is how bad I feel ☐

I'll do anything to avoid feeling distressed and upset ☐

I can't stand having these feelings ☐

It's weak and pathetic to feel so upset ☐

I hate myself for feeling like this, like I've failed ☐

These feelings will go on for ever if I don't do something ☐

Other people seem to be able to tolerate being upset much better than I can ☐

Sometimes I feel numb, empty or cut off from my feelings ☐

If you ticked more than one or two of these items, then it's likely that you do struggle to face your feelings.

What happens if you don't face your feelings?

You might ask, 'What's wrong with trying to avoid feelings? They're horrible, and they don't do any good, do they? Why shouldn't I avoid them?' The problem is that a lot of the strategies you use to avoid the feelings can create new problems for you. Most escape strategies have a downside, unfortunately, as shown below.

Escape strategy	Downside
Drink a lot or take a lot of drugs	Get addicted to drugs and alcohol
Cut myself to replace emotional pain with physical one	Cause myself damage and embarrassment if I need hospital treatment. Piss everyone off. Need to be careful what I wear
Take it out on other people	Lose friends, become isolated
Avoid people and situations	End up with no friends, and a very restricted life
Binge eat	Mess up body chemistry and weight
Spend too much money	Get into debt
Be promiscuous	Put myself at risk of being hurt or getting ill

The trouble about these methods is that although they work in the short term – all of them *do* help you avoid or escape from distress – they backfire and make things worse in the long term, as shown in Figure 4. And what's more, all the downsides described above are likely to cause you *new* distressing emotions, and then you have to cope with those, too.

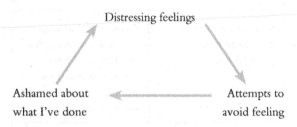

Fig. 4 The effect of escape strategies

There's another downside as well, which is that because you use these unhelpful strategies you don't learn to cope with the emotions in a more helpful way. If you can learn to use more helpful strategies, then the picture will look more like Figure 5:

Distressing feelings
easier to deal with

Distressing
feelings

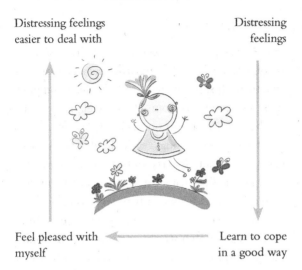

Feel pleased with ◄━━━━━━━━━ Learn to cope
myself   in a good way

Fig. 5 Helpful coping strategies

So what's needed?

The upshot of this is that, no matter how difficult
and impossible it seems, we need to learn to cope
with our emotions in a more helpful way. You
might be thinking, 'They must be joking, I could
never do any of this, and none of it will work,' and
it's true that it can be *very* difficult to believe it can
make a difference. But if you try, and if you have
someone to support you, then you might find that
coping with feelings *can* get easier.

Accepting feelings

Strange though it may seem, one of the best ways to tolerate negative feelings is to accept that you have them. Instead of trying to fight them and push them away, remind yourself that feelings are part of what human beings normally experience. If we didn't have any feelings, we'd hardly be human. You are not mad, or crazy, or bad, to feel as you do. Some people find that it can help to have a sentence or two prepared for when they feel overwhelmed. You could write these down, or write something similar in your own words, and carry them around with you so that you have them to hand when you need them. Here are a couple of examples:

> 'I hate these feelings, but I know it makes sense that I feel them, given what's happened to me. I know that if I can just hang on they will go away in the end.'

> 'I know that I experience emotion much more strongly than other people do. I'm not crazy or weak, it's just more of a struggle for me.'

Accepting distress doesn't mean that you like having the feelings. But ask yourself whether trying to fight them and push them away has worked for you. If you are reading this then it's quite likely that it hasn't. When you feel yourself trying to escape from the emotion in one of the self-destructive ways we described earlier, take a step back and let yourself think for a minute. Instead of reaching for the bottle or the razor blade, remember the things that we've spoken about.

If you have read Part 1 of this book, then you will have learned a bit about emotions, but if you haven't then we will summarise the important points here:

- **Emotions are normal.** We all have them, even though for some people they are particularly extreme. In fact, we think that there's something wrong with people who *don't* experience emotions – we might comment that someone didn't seem to care when their spouse died, or that someone said they weren't scared when they were trapped in a fire.

- **Emotions are useful.** They help to protect us, and help us to survive. For example, fear helps us to fight or run away fast, anger helps us to stand up for ourselves, sadness helps us to let other people know that we need caring for.

- **Emotions developed over a long period of time in our evolution.** This means that some of our emotions are very primitive, and some are more sophisticated. Some of us are much more susceptible to extreme emotions because this was a way in which our tribe or troop was able to survive.

So an alternative way in which you can try to accept emotions is just to remind yourself that they are normal and useful, and that we wouldn't be human if we didn't have them.

Another way to accept feelings is to learn to stand back from them. This approach comes from the ideas of mindfulness, but you don't have to take on the whole of mindfulness in order to use some of the strategies. Both of the techniques below can help you to stand back.

- **Describe your feelings.** Try to stand back from emotions by describing them to yourself: 'I'm feeling a churning in my stomach, and I'm thinking that this will never end.' Don't judge or criticise yourself for having these feelings, just describe them.

- **Visualise your emotions.** Some people find it helps to have a visual image of emotions. You can imagine your emotions as if they are storm clouds in the sky, churning away and looking very fierce, while you are on the ground watching. Alternatively, there's a turbulent river and you are in the middle of it, being smashed on the rocks and pulled underwater. Now try to imagine that you are sitting on the bank of the river watching it go by. It's still crashing on the rocks and churning everything around, but you are not *in* it – you're just watching it.

Strategies to help you cope with distress

Even if you've got very good at accepting your feelings, there are still times when it would be good to try to stop yourself feeling so bad. In this section we'll describe some strategies that you can use.

Distraction

Very often there are powerful vicious cycles involved in emotion. For example, if you can feel your heart beating, you might think, 'Oh no, my heart is beating too hard, I'm going to have a heart attack and die.' That's a really frightening thought, so your body will respond by producing adrenaline, which makes your heart beat faster, and then your thoughts get even worse.

Since it is *so* common for emotions to follow this pattern of a vicious cycle, we need to learn how to break into the cycle. Since thoughts play such a powerful role in the cycle, then one way in which we can help is to give our attention to something else, so that our thoughts can't keep going round and round. This is the essence of distraction. Distraction can be unhelpful if we use it all the time, but it can be an extremely good strategy when we need to get out of our vicious cycles. All the different things that we suggest here have an element of distraction to them, in that they all draw our attention away from ourselves, but there are some things that you can do more directly, just to distract yourself. For example, try doing crossword puzzles or Sudoku. Or mental arithmetic – try counting backwards in threes from 1001. It takes a surprising amount of concentration to do it. Or you could try writing down all the meals you've had in the last week. How many vegetables have you eaten?

There are many such things that you can do, so make a list opposite of all the things that you think might help you and keep it with you, or stick it on the fridge, so you can see it quickly when you need it. Afterwards make a note of whether those things helped or not. If not, then write down something different to try. If so, then well done, and carry on!

Distracting things I can try	How it went

Alternatives to self-destructive behaviours

The suggestions that we have included below are all things that people have told us about and said that they've helped. They might sound a bit strange, but it's definitely worth giving them a go. They may be helpful if you think you're about to do something like binge, or cut yourself.

Ice cubes

- Surprisingly helpful! Get some ice cubes from the fridge and smash them into the bath. It's very satisfying.

- Get hold of an ice cube and squeeze it in your hand so that your hand goes numb.

- Try rubbing an ice cube on your lower forehead, just above your nose.

Senses

Try to use your senses to distract yourself from your emotions. For example:

- Put English mustard on your thumb and rub it on the roof of your mouth.

- Chew a chilli and then swallow it.

- Put an elastic band on your wrist and snap it every time you think of harming yourself.

- Scream into a pillow as loudly as you can.

- Use a red pen and draw marks on your skin where you'd otherwise have cut.

- Cut up an onion so you start crying – crying is actually quite good for you because it releases stress hormones.

Get yourself out of the physical environment that you're in

Often we tend to self-harm in the same location. This is frequently somewhere in our own homes, maybe the bedroom or bathroom if we live with other people. If we are away from home when we start feeling distressed, then we might try to get back as soon as possible so that we can self-harm. Other popular places might be the loos at work or at college.

If you are in a physical environment where you have self-harmed before, it's much more likely that you will do it again. Get yourself out if at all possible! Take yourself to a place where it would be much harder – go and sit in the cinema if you can afford it, or ride a bike, or just walk around for a bit. If you live in the country, go and find an empty field and scream. If you are away from your self-harming place when the urge starts, then try as hard as you can to stay away until the urge has begun to die down.

Try to speak to someone

We know that when you are on the point of self-harming, then it's really difficult to make a phone call and ask for help. But it can be helpful to think in advance about who you *might* be able to talk to. Write the names and numbers down and keep them with you, so that you don't have to decide who to get in touch with when you feel bad. You already know that these are good options. We give more information in the resources section at the end of the book, but here are some ideas:

- the Samaritans – call 116 123;

- your mental health team, or their out-of-hours contacts;

- the GP out-of-hours number.

Concentrate on someone else

This can be a really good way to distract yourself,

because it not only diverts you from your feelings but can make you feel good about yourself too. Do something for someone else:

- Call voluntary organisations – soup kitchens or homeless shelters, or charity shops – and ask if you can do something for them.

- Call friends or family and ask if they need help doing anything. Say you're bored and looking for something to do.

- Do something simple like make a cup of tea for someone.

Or take your attention off yourself:

- Go and walk round a shopping centre or park, and watch the people there. Make up stories about their lives. Do they look happy or sad? Have they just won the lottery? Are they on the way to the solicitor to talk about their divorce? What advice would you give them about their clothes? What help might they like with their lives?

- Name five colours that you can see, four things you can hear, three things you can smell, two things you can touch, and one thing you can taste!

- Think of someone you care about, and keep a picture of them in your wallet. Take the picture out and ask them what they'd do in a situation like this. Ask them how they are.

Look through the lists above and write down opposite some things that you think would be worth trying. When you've had a go, make a note about whether they have helped. If not, then pick another one for next time.

Opposite action

We've talked about the way in which trying to avoid and escape from emotions can have downsides and end up being very self-destructive. Sometimes the way that we cope with emotions is by *acting* on them. If we are angry, we shout or hit out; we want to hurt someone physically or mentally. If we are frightened, we run away, or freeze. Not only do these ways of behaving cause problems later, but they also *intensify* the original feeling and make it much stronger and longer lasting. The more you act on the emotion, the stronger it gets. So we can try to reverse this cycle. It follows that if we do the opposite of what the emotion is telling us to do, it should start to die down. So 'opposite action' – although it sounds very contradictory – can be a good way to cope without inviting negative consequences.

Things I could try	How they worked
_____	_____
_____	_____
_____	_____
_____	_____
_____	_____
_____	_____
_____	_____
_____	_____
_____	_____
_____	_____
_____	_____
_____	_____
_____	_____
_____	_____
_____	_____
_____	_____
_____	_____
_____	_____
_____	_____
_____	_____
_____	_____

> **Note: It is extremely important to be aware that this does not mean that your emotion isn't real, or that you shouldn't be feeling it. It's about acknowledging the emotion and trying to regulate it.**

For example, imagine that you are afraid of spiders, and that you see a huge spider in a cupboard when you are looking for your old coat; you are likely to back off in a hurry and slam the cupboard door. But does this make the fear go away? In fact it makes it worse, so next time you might not even be able to open the cupboard door; you might need to find someone to do it for you. The emotion-driven behaviour intensifies your fear.

Now imagine standing at the door of the cupboard and looking at the spider. Study it as closely as you can manage. For example, what colour is it? Although your fear might be very intense at the beginning, you should notice that it dies down.

This is opposite action: it's the basis of a lot of treatments for anxiety, and it works for other emotions, too. Have a look at the summary in the box opposite.

Emotion	Emotion-driven behaviour	Opposite action	Impact on emotion with opposite action
Angry	Shout, attack, criticise, physically hurt	Try to understand why the person did what they did. Speak quietly	Anger dies down. Feel more sympathy for the person who made you angry
Sad	Withdraw, be passive, slump	Get involved, be active. Stand straight	Sadness lessens. Feel more energised or motivated
Upset	Use alcohol and drugs to escape	Don't numb distressing feelings. Allow yourself to feel them, and do things that are soothing in a good way, or which will get you active (see sections on pleasurable activities and relaxation)	Upset dies down; no drug or alcohol hangover. Feel better about yourself

To plan for opposite action, it helps to think ahead. What are common emotions for you? How do you normally cope with them? Try doing the opposite action instead, and afterwards fill out the form below:

What are my trigger situations – the times when I know I'm likely to feel very emotional?

_____

_____

_____

_____

_____

What do I usually feel?

_____

_____

_____

_____

_____

What emotion-driven behaviour do
I want to adopt?

_____

_____

_____

_____

What problems does this usually lead to?

_____

_____

_____

_____

_____

What opposite action could I do instead?

_____

_____

_____

_____

_____

What impact did it have on my emotions?

_____

_____

_____

_____

_____

Problem solving

Although most of us can solve a lot of problems quite easily, when we get very distressed our ability to think clearly disintegrates completely, and we become unable to solve the easiest puzzle. Remember that we described in Part 1 how our emotion brain switches our thinking brain off? As you become better at calming and soothing yourself, then it will be easier to think about problems. The process laid out in the following box will help remind you of what needs to be done.

1 *Define the problem*

This sounds surprisingly obvious, but often when your emotions are aroused it's hard even to see what the problem is. Try to write it down as clearly as you can.

2 *Break the problem down into small parts*

Sometimes a problem is quite a complex thing! Think of all the different aspects of the problem, and write these down too.

3 *Think of all possible solutions*

Even if some of the solutions you come up with are daft and you 'know' they won't work, write them down anyway. Writing down crazy solutions will free your mind. Think of what the cleverest person in the world might come up with.

4 *Think of the pros and cons of each solution*

Go through each of the solutions you've written down and write down the pros and cons of each. Think of whether you have the resources needed. Do you need help from other people to carry them out? Are there people you could ask? Are some of them more comfortable for you than others?

5 *Choose a solution*

Once you have been through all the pros and cons, then pick the one that seems most feasible for you. Once you've chosen, then commit to it – this is what you are going to do! Go through the solution and make sure you know exactly when and how you are going to do it. If the solution has a number of different steps to it, then write these down separately so you know where you are.

6 *Carry it out*

Start the action!

7 *Review and evaluate*

Once you have carried out your course of action, then review how it went. Have you sorted the problem out? Completely? Partially? If so, then very well done! If not, then go back to your list. What else could you try?

Don't dismiss distress tolerance!

Think of the impact of what you feel like doing when you are overwhelmed by powerful emotions. Often when you are in a state of great upset, you just want to do something – anything – to make it better. In that moment you don't really care about what effect your actions are going to have on the people around you, or even on yourself. You might think things like this:

'I feel so awful that nothing matters –
nothing could be worse than this.'

'I'm so bad – doing bad things to myself
is what I deserve.'

'Nobody cares about me anyway, so why
would they care what I do?'

'He's just looking for an excuse to leave
me, so I'll give him one.'

This means that it's very unlikely you'll want to try any of the possible solutions we've discussed, and you certainly won't believe that they'll make any difference. You just want the pain to go away. So it's extremely hard to convince yourself that it's worth trying anything different.

But even though you are feeling desperate, try to remember how things have turned out in the past. Try to remind yourself that they can turn out better, and make a plan for what you can do.

Write out a statement to help you keep in mind that it's worth trying. You could carry this around with you, as with the statements at the end of the section on 'Crises and self-harm'. Maybe something like this:

'It is normal and acceptable for me to
feel like this. I'm not crazy or evil. Just

because I'm trying to cope with emotions
in a different way doesn't mean that they
don't count.'

Hang on to this thought, and make a plan following
the steps below:

Distress tolerance plan

Situations that often make me very distressed

_____

_____

_____

_____

_____

_____

What I normally do to cope

_____

_____

_____

_____

_____

_____

How I feel afterwards

_____

_____

_____

_____

_____

_____

What I am going to try to do differently

_____

_____

_____

_____

_____

_____

How I feel afterwards

_____

_____

_____

_____

_____

_____

Next steps

_____

_____

_____

_____

_____

_____

8

Regulating your emotions

We've covered crises and times of great distress, but learning to regulate more everyday emotions can be helpful, too. This chapter covers skills that can be used not just in extreme cases, but every day, to help you to learn about and regulate your emotions when you're feeling calmer. Some of the distress tolerance techniques we've already explored, such as problem solving and mindfulness, can also come in useful here.

Emotion regulation skills involve a combination of recognising and accepting emotions while also changing the ways in which you respond to them. This is what Marsha Linehan, who developed Dialectical Behaviour Therapy, means by 'dialectic'. Rather than arguing whether acceptance or change is the right thing to do, she recognises that both views are valid, and tries to bring them together.

Strategies to help regulate your emotions

Recognising and labelling emotions

Learning to recognise, label and describe what is going on inside you is an important first step to being able to reduce the intensity of your emotions and the effect they can have on you. Although it may seem strange, learning to label and describe emotions can really help you to stand back from how you feel.

It may be very hard for you to do this at first. If we think back to the idea that people who struggle with emotions were probably never taught how to handle them, then it's likely that you don't *know* exactly what you're feeling. For instance, imagine you were upset that your older sibling had gone to school for the first time while you were still at home. As a young child you'd have needed someone to say, 'I know you feel sad, but it's OK – she'll be back later.' So the upset started to feel a bit more manageable.

If this didn't happen, then all you know about is the upset, without having words to describe it, or ways to understand it. If you are very susceptible to strong emotions, then it might have been extremely difficult to understand and cope with how you were feeling.

This means that now you have to learn to do all this for yourself. It might be difficult, but it's also very helpful, if you are in a situation which frequently triggers strong emotions in you. You've got to learn things now that you should have been taught years ago!

To start learning how to do this, take a recent emotional situation and fill in the 'Labelling your emotions' chart opposite as fully as you can. Then, for at least two weeks, complete one of these charts each time a strong emotion gets triggered.

Labelling your emotions

Situation: Where was I? Who was around?
What just happened?

_____

_____

_____

_____

_____

What I feel in my body:

_____

_____

_____

_____

_____

What I feel in my mind:

_____

_____

_____

_____

_____

What I want to do (i.e. what actions do
I want to perform):

_____

_____

_____

_____

_____

And therefore, what is a possible description
of how I feel?

_____

_____

_____

_____

_____

We have included an example below from Maggie, who became very emotional when she saw a picture of two of her friends having coffee without her.

Situation:

Saw a Facebook picture of Sam and Jess having coffee at the new place – they hadn't asked me if I wanted to go.

What I feel in my body:

Hot, flushed, sweaty.

What I feel in my mind:

Horrible, painful, want to burst into tears and scream. Think they don't like me or ever want me around.

What actions do I want to perform?

Ring them up and shout at them. Tell them I don't care about them, either.

And therefore, what is a possible description of how I feel?

It feels like rage – and it is, but I think it could also be described as jealous and disappointed.

To see if doing this helps you, make a rough estimate of how bad your emotion is before and after you've filled in the chart. Here are the steps:

Step 1: Before you fill in the chart, rate how strong your emotion is on the scale below

0	1	2	3	4	5	6	7	8	9	10

No emotion   Worst emotion ever

Step 2: Fill in the emotion chart

Step 3: Rate how strong your emotion is after you've filled in the chart

0	1	2	3	4	5	6	7	8	9	10

No emotion   Worst emotion ever

Hopefully after you have done this for a couple of weeks, you should see that the strength of your emotion has decreased a lot after you have filled in the chart.

Note too that with this chart we are not asking you to argue against the emotion – just to get a good handle on what that horrible morass of feeling is made up of.

Mindfulness: becoming more aware of your emotions

Mindfulness is a technique that enables us to experience things without judging them, and without being caught up in them in an unhelpful way. It's a way of becoming aware of what you are doing and feeling, learning to watch it rather than getting swept up in it. The development of mindfulness was spearheaded by an American scientist called Jon Kabat-Zinn, who was interested in the practice of Buddhist meditation, and started to use it to help many of his patients, particularly those who were experiencing a lot of physical pain. He found that learning to meditate greatly reduced the amount of stress that people experienced, and helped patients suffering pain to cope with it much better. Hearing about his work, people across the world became interested in how this could be used, and the practice of mindfulness developed. Mindfulness is not quite the same as Buddhist meditation, and you don't have to be a Buddhist to use it. It's been shown to be really effective at helping people to cope with how they feel, and increasing their psychological well-being.

This section does not teach you how to become skilled at mindful meditation, but we can start with some simple strategies. If you want to learn more, then there are resources and reading suggested at the end of the book. However, you can become more mindful of your emotional reactions to certain situations and improve your observational skills in the moment. This may help you to slow down your emotional responses and become less caught up in your urges to react. Some people find the ideas below helpful.

Practising mindfulness

Mindfulness is an ordinary experience of choosing to place our awareness on the present moment, while gently acknowledging and accepting our feelings, thoughts and bodily sensations. By being fully present in this way – not pushing feelings away or avoiding them, but actually being with them – we create space to respond in new ways to situations and make wise choices.

It may take time and practice to develop a personal understanding of mindfulness, but there is no right or wrong experience. It can be helpful to establish a consistent place to practise, perhaps a chair in the corner of your bedroom, study or lounge. Initially you can begin with 3–5 minutes twice a day.

'Check in' with yourself. What emotions are you aware of? What thoughts are going through your head? What feelings or sensations are arising in your body? How are you feeling generally? Accept what arises without reacting or responding. Whatever is there is neither good nor bad. Watch your thoughts and feelings and choose to let them go. This will become easier with practice, and self-compassion is important. If you find yourself following a thought stream for a while, gently bring your attention back to your breath.

The following sample exercise shows you how to begin. (It's taken from *Mindfulness: A Practical Guide to Finding Peace in a Frantic World*. You can find more information on this at www.franticworld.com

Three-minute Breathing Space meditation

Step 1: Becoming aware

Deliberately adopt an erect and dignified posture, whether sitting or standing. If possible, close your eyes. Then, bring your awareness to your inner experience and acknowledge it, asking: what is my experience right now?

- What *thoughts* are going through the mind? As best you can, acknowledge thoughts as mental events.

- What *feelings* are here? Turn towards any sense of discomfort or unpleasant feelings, acknowledging them without trying to make them different from how you find them.

- What *body sensations* are here right now? Perhaps quickly scan the body to pick up any sensations of tightness or bracing, acknowledging the sensations, but, once again, not trying to change them in any way.

Step 2: Gathering and focusing attention

Now, redirecting the attention to a narrow 'spotlight' on the physical sensations of the breath, move in close to the physical sensations of the breath in the abdomen . . . expanding as the breath comes in . . . and falling back as the breath goes out. Follow the breath all the way in and all the way out. Use each breath as an opportunity to anchor yourself into the present. And if the mind wanders, gently escort the attention back to the breath.

Step 3: Expanding attention

Now, expand the field of awareness around the breathing so that it includes a sense of the body as a whole, your posture and facial expression, as if the whole body was breathing. If you become aware of any sensations of discomfort, tension, feel free to bring your focus of attention right in to the intensity by imagining that the breath could move into and around the sensations. In this, you are helping to explore the sensations, befriending them, rather than trying to change them in any way. If they stop pulling for your attention, return to sitting, aware of the whole body, moment by moment.

We can also begin to create mindfulness moments in our everyday lives; noticing while having a shower what the water feels like as it touches our skin, exploring the first few sips of morning coffee or tea and being aware of the taste and experience. Some people may choose to attend mindfulness groups to provide support for their practice, and to aid motivation and inspiration to keep it going as they begin to see the benefits. This can offer you the opportunity to learn new exercises, practise mindful movement and maybe attend longer periods of mindfulness practice.

Trying pleasurable activities

Strange though it may seem, sometimes doing pleasurable activities can make a difference, even if you think you're feeling much too bad to try. The idea is not wait to do something that is pleasurable until you feel good, but to take action to change how you are feeling. There are some suggestions below, but there may be many others that you can think of once you start:

- Eat a chocolate bar (though only if bingeing isn't an issue for you!).

- Go for a bike ride or a walk.

- Text a mate.

- Watch a funny film or TV programme.

- Exercise.

- Go to a bookshop and read or have a cup of coffee.

- Listen to upbeat music.

- Paint your nails.

- Take a long bath.

- Draw a picture.

- Read a celebrity magazine.

- Sign up to learn a new language.

- Look at your favourite websites.

- Write a letter to yourself as if you were some-one who wanted to cheer you up.

Make a note of things that you think it might be worth trying, and then once you've done them write down whether they helped or not:

Things I could try	How they worked

Self-soothing and relaxation

Very often, people who have problems with their emotions have never learned how to calm and soothe themselves in a good way. Self-soothing is about comforting yourself, being nurturing to yourself, and being compassionate and kind. Self-soothing also helps our bodies to calm down and relax, so that they in turn help our feelings to calm down instead of making them more keyed up.

We tend to talk about self-soothing by using our senses – sight, hearing, touch, taste and smell. All of these can be used.

- *Sight*: look at something that you think looks beautiful or interesting. You might like looking at trees and plants, or at art books; at pictures of houses or interiors, or animals.

- *Hearing:* listen to sounds that you enjoy. Music is the most obvious thing, but there may also be other sounds – the wind blowing through trees, birds calling. Some people find the sound of whale noises extremely enjoyable.

- *Touch:* many people find that stroking and soothing their pet can soothe them. Have a bath or a shower and concentrate on the feeling of the water or the flannel on your body, or hold a hot mug of tea or coffee. Carry something soft and velvety around with you, so that you can stroke or feel it when you need to. Wrap yourself in a blanket with a hot water bottle.

* *Taste:* drink a cup of tea or hot chocolate slowly and let yourself concentrate on the taste. Unless eating is a problem for you, carry sweets or lollipops with you. When you eat or drink, concentrate on the taste sensations.

* *Smell:* buy scented candles or incense. Go to the perfume counter of a big shop and try loads of different smells. Put a favourite smell on a hanky and keep it with you so that the smell will comfort you when you need it.

Things I could try	How it went

Cue-controlled relaxation

When you have found things that soothe you and help you to relax, then think of a word or phrase that will summarise what you've been doing – maybe the name of your pet, or a line from a piece of music. Or it could be a word like 'relax' or 'peace'. Think of the word or phrase when you know that you are feeling soothed and relaxed. Then, at other times when you are out and about, just thinking of the word can bring back some of the feelings of relaxation.

Safe place visualisation

Rather like cue-controlled relaxation, this is a technique that involves calling something into your mind that helps you to feel calm and safe. Think of somewhere which makes you feel calm and relaxed. This might be a real place where you have felt safe in the past, or it might be an imaginary place. It could be a beach, or a park, or a wood. It could be a room high above a city where you can look down on the life below.

Once you have decided what your safe place is going to be, then find somewhere quiet and comfortable where you can sit and not be disturbed. Make sure that you are sitting comfortably, and close your eyes. Take long slow breaths in and out, and breathe slowly and gently throughout the exercise.

• With your eyes closed, imagine that you are in your safe place. Think first about what you can see. What's around you, what does it look like? Is it day or night? Choose something soothing in your safe place to concentrate on for a few seconds. It might be a plant or a picture.

• Now think of what you can hear. You might hear the rush of wind through the trees, or traffic far below you. You might hear music or laughter. Let yourself concentrate on a soothing sound.

• Do the same thing for your sense of touch and smell and taste. If you're walking on the beach, can you feel the gritty sand under your feet, and smell the sea?

• As you imagine all of these sensations, let yourself feel calm and relaxed, and recognise how safe you feel here. Remember that you can come back to this place in your imagination any time you want to!

My emotion regulation plan

Once you've finished reading this section, you might like to try filling in the following table, which may help to bring together everything you've learned.

Situations that make me very emotional:

_____

_____

_____

_____

What I normally do to cope:

_____

_____

_____

_____

How I feel afterwards:

_____

_____

_____

_____

What I am going to try to do differently:

_____

_____

_____

_____

How I feel afterwards:

_____

_____

_____

_____

Next steps:

_____

_____

_____

_____

9

Supporting your recovery

Why is how you live so important to getting better?

Most people would feel bad if they didn't eat properly, or slept at erratic times, or didn't know what to do with themselves during the day, or drank too much. For people with BPD it can be very hard to care about getting day-to-day life in order, but at the same time it's even more important, because living erratically really messes with your mood. So you need to try to manage your basic needs, establish routines, and find a fit in the external world.

Of course, this may be easier said than done. Part of the problem may be that you have never learned how to do it, because when you were younger the people around you did not show you how to. Your parents may have responded to your basic needs inconsistently, failing, perhaps, to feed you regularly or to make sure you were in bed at the right time. They may have been absent without giving you any explanation, and left you to fend for yourself. They may have imposed routine and structure on you randomly, or without any concern for what was right for you.

Another problem is not just that you never learned to look after yourself, but that when you try to do so it feels really boring! Impulsivity and recklessness are undoubtedly more fun. Being sensible can make you feel numb and dead inside, and this can be very difficult to tolerate. Nevertheless, living a regular life really can help your recovery.

What does recovery from personality disorder mean?

As mental health services have changed, there has been a big move to think about recovery. Recovery emphasises that it's not just medication that helps in treatment, and that people are more than their diagnosis. Recovery means a process in which the person takes charge of their life and lives as full and rich a life as they can, despite their symptoms or problems.

Recovery is an individualised process and involves different goals and activities for different people, but the basic principle is the same – to live as fulfilling a life as you can, despite your difficulties, and not to let the difficulties define you. Recovery can include:

- reclaiming control over your life, and having real choice about treatment and care;

- rebuilding positive personal and social identity;

- developing relationships and a sense of connectedness with the world around you;

- developing hope and optimism about the future;

- finding meaning and purpose in your life.

But this can seem very daunting. Many of us struggle at times to achieve fulfilment in life, so for people with extreme emotions or BPD it's likely to be even harder. Often people with personality disorder see the external world as a very hostile place (and not without reason!) and feel very isolated and alienated from it. It is not hard to imagine how some of the processes of recovery might feel very difficult if this is how you experience the world and your place in it. So what is important is that you should find a way to live in and relate to the external world without having to resort to withdrawal or self-harm in order to feel safe. The following processes may be particularly important:

- developing acceptance of who you are;

- taking care of yourself;

- understanding and managing your emotions;

- improving your relationships and who you spend time with;

- claiming a place in your community and finding purpose.

We have talked about managing your emotions in the sections on distress tolerance and regulating emotions. We are going to look at three of the other processes here: developing acceptance of who you are, taking care of yourself, and finding purpose in life.

Developing acceptance of who you are

Kindness
is the most important
superpower

People with extreme emotions or BPD can find it very difficult to be around others, but they can also find it difficult to be around themselves, and find it hard to spend time on their own. That kind of makes sense – being with yourself, if you don't like yourself, is just as bad as being with someone else you don't like! So how can you begin the monumental task of learning to like and accept yourself?

One very straightforward way is to treat yourself well. Imagine that you spent all day with someone who said, 'You're so ugly and repulsive. No one likes you. You're really stupid, you're just an embarrassment.' By the end of the day you would be very likely to feel absolutely dreadful. Now imagine that you spent all day with someone who said, 'You're getting on well today. The people in that support group seemed to like you. You said some really helpful things at that meeting.' By the end of the day you'd probably be feeling quite good about yourself. The same applies if the person saying all this stuff is you – if you tell yourself you're rubbish, you'll feel rubbish. If you tell yourself you're doing well, you'll feel that you are.

If you have BPD, it's much more likely that you will have spent your life being told you're rubbish, first in your childhood, and then possibly because you choose people who do the same when you're an adult. But here is the crucial point: *Don't join in! Just because other people have bullied and abused you, it doesn't mean that you have to do it, too.* Other people may have been horrible to you because they are horrible, or have problems of their own. You don't need to do it as well.

Of course, it will be difficult for you to believe this. But, for the moment, don't even spend time thinking about it. Just make the decision: I am going to be kind to myself. Then stick to it. Here are some practical ways to do it:

- Give yourself compliments. It doesn't matter if you don't believe them at first; just do it. They don't have to be big things, either – making a cup of tea would do it. You could say, 'That was really good – you didn't even want to get out of bed, but you have got up and made tea. Well done.'

- Write a list of your good points. Start with just three, and add to them later. If you can't think of three, then ask someone else – a friend, or a therapist or other professional. Also, the good points don't have to be super-good. You don't have to be the best in the world at something (no, you really don't) for it to count.

- For both of the above, keep a notebook, or an electronic record, so you can look at it when you feel low. Or keep a 'positives jar' – weird, you might think, but some people find it useful. Write down good things about yourself on bits of paper and put them in a jar. When you feel awful, take a piece of paper out and have a look.

- Catch yourself when you are telling yourself how awful you are and tell your bully self to shut up!

- Give yourself treats. Wine gums, chocolates (as long as chocolate isn't a problem area for you), scented things in the bath or shower, flowers. Be nice to yourself.

It will feel really strange and difficult to do these things, but they do honestly make a difference if you keep going, and after a while it might start to sink in that you really do deserve to be treated this way!

Taking care of yourself

The next way that you can be kind to yourself is by taking care of yourself properly. This may be something else that didn't happen when you were a child, and it's possible that no one else has done it either. But again, just because other people didn't take care of you, it doesn't mean that you shouldn't take care of yourself. Of course, it might take a bit of learning – you might not really know what taking care of yourself means. But here are some of the areas that you can think about.

Eating well

One of the easiest ways to neglect yourself is by not eating properly – going without food for long periods of time, or eating excessively regardless of your feelings of hunger. Both of these will disrupt your body's metabolism and digestion, and mess with your sugar and energy levels, your concentration, menstruation (in women) and feelings of well-being. So eating well can be a really good start. Remember that your body needs three meals a day, and needs a good balance of protein, complex carbohydrates, and fruit and vegetables.

Think about how you eat, and about whether you are making life more difficult for yourself by eating badly. Do you think you could improve your diet? If so, what would be the advantages and difficulties of doing this? Write down any ideas you have overleaf.

Advantages	Difficulties
_____	_____
_____	_____
_____	_____
_____	_____
_____	_____
_____	_____
_____	_____
_____	_____
_____	_____
_____	_____
_____	_____
_____	_____
_____	_____
_____	_____
_____	_____
_____	_____
_____	_____
_____	_____
_____	_____

Now think about what you could do differently –
you don't have to do everything at once, but just
start to make some changes and see how you feel.
Try eating an apple a day (after all, it is meant to
keep the doctor away), or cutting down on the
twenty cups of coffee that make you twitchy and
unable to sleep. Keep a note of them in the box
below.

My first changes will be:

1 _____

_____

_____

_____

_____

_____

_____

2 _____

_____

_____

_____

_____

_____

_____

3 _____

_____

_____

_____

_____

_____

_____

Finding the right level of activity

We all need to find the right balance between activity and rest. For almost everyone, too little activity makes you feel bored and depressed; too much activity makes you feel stressed and exhausted.

Research into depression has shown that finding a balance between activities that give you a sense of mastery (achievement) and pleasure can make a difference to your mood and well-being. Psychologists use the term 'behavioural activation' to describe an approach that concentrates on increasing these activities, and have shown that it can be as good as a course of therapy.

It's helpful to think of activity in terms of a number of different areas:

- *Basic jobs*, such as washing up, shopping. Probably not that pleasurable, but hopefully doing these things will give you a sense of achievement.

- *Physical activity* – tempting though it is, lying on the sofa all day is not going to make you feel great. Physical activity doesn't have to be extreme exercise; any kind of walking, or even vigorous housework, will be fine.

- *Relaxation* – this counts as an activity if you're doing it on purpose. Lying on the sofa because you can't face getting up *doesn't* count, but sitting down with the paper and a cup of tea does.

* *Purposeful activity* – we will say more about this in the section below, but purposeful activity, and the goals that go with it, can make an enormous difference to how you feel.

Another aspect of activity is that it can be very helpful to have structure and routine in your day, and to plan when you are going to do each activity. This is especially important if you don't have any kind of external structure in your life, like a job, or any kind of commitment. Too much unstructured time is a bit of a risk for anyone. Sometimes structure and routine can feel alienating and boring, but it can really help, especially on days when you are feeling low and can't be bothered.

Think about how you spend your day. Is there a balance between the different kinds of activities? If changing your level of activity feels like a big task, think about the advantages and difficulties of doing so. (For example, why might you find routines difficult to stick to?)

Changing your level of activity	
Advantages	**Difficulties**

Now you have looked at the advantages and disadvantages, and hopefully decided that you do want to make changes, what is your plan? Remember that you don't need to change everything at once – just start with small changes and see if it makes a difference to how you feel.

My first changes will be:

1 _____

_____

_____

_____

_____

_____

2 _____

_____

_____

_____

_____

_____

_____

_____

3 _____

_____

_____

_____

_____

_____

_____

Sleep

Sleep can have a huge impact on how we feel. A good night's sleep can make us feel great, while a lack of sleep can really drag us down and make us feel low, irritable, unable to concentrate. Sometimes when people can't sleep, it's very tempting to use drugs or alcohol to help, or to use sleeping tablets or other sedative medication. While these things can be helpful in the short term, they don't really solve the problem. Sleeping tablets are almost all addictive, and their effects wear off after a short time. Sometimes people find when they are unable to sleep at night that they may start to sleep in the day, which then makes going to sleep at night even more problematic. Your diet and activity levels will also play a part in your body's ability to sleep, so addressing the other areas mentioned in this chapter is important, too.

There are a number of different strategies that you can use to try to help with your sleep, known as 'sleep hygiene'. Here are some of the things that you can try:

- Make sure that you don't drink a lot of tea and coffee in the late afternoon and evening.

- Don't use alcohol to help you sleep – what normally happens is that you get off to sleep OK, but then wake in the early hours of the morning feeling dreadful.

- Don't use too much technology in the evening. The light from laptops and other devices is so bright that it makes your brain think that it's midday – no wonder it doesn't want to sleep.

- Make your room comfortable and nice to be in. A lot of people are affected by clutter and mess, even without realising it.

- If your bedroom is noisy, or too light, and there's nothing you can do about it because it's the fault of your house mates or neighbours, then buy earplugs and eye pads – they're worth investing in.

- Don't do anything in bed (apart from the obvious) other than read a bit. Your bed is the place where you sleep, not eat, play Angry Birds, etc.

- If you are having problems sleeping, don't stay in bed. Get up for ten minutes and do something different – wait until you feel sleepy before you go back to bed.

- If you are worrying and fretting, write what's worrying you down on a piece of paper and tell yourself that you'll think about it in the morning.

- Remember that everything always seems worse at night.

Think about which of these strategies might be helpful for you, and make a plan for change:

My first changes will be:

1 _____

_____

_____

_____

_____

_____

_____

2 _____

_____

_____

_____

_____

3 _____

_____

_____

_____

_____

_____

_____

Finding a purpose and developing a role

If you've been struggling just to survive in life, it might seem almost impossible to think about meaning and purpose. It might be too tough to imagine feeling purposeful! And yet, there may be something that you care about, or that you'd like to do if only you didn't feel so awful. There might be something that you've done in the past but given up on because you felt you couldn't cope. It can be really hard to think of things like that out of the blue, but it might help to ask yourself how important certain areas of your life are.

Look at the list overleaf. Which of these are *most* important or interesting to you? If you could do something in any of these areas, would that seem valuable to you? Would it give you a sense of meaning? Are there glaring omissions that make you think, 'Why didn't they put that in?'

Rank these in ascending order, from least important to most important:

☐ Relationships: partner, children, parents, siblings, friends, etc.

☐ Work and career

☐ Education/training/personal growth

☐ Being creative

☐ Spirituality

☐ Connecting with nature

☐ Helping others

☐ Caring for the environment

☐ Healthy living

☐ Caring for animals

Now look at the things that you've scored highest in the list, and choose the one or two that are most important. Then think about what makes them important to you, and write them down opposite.

Most important areas

_____

_____

_____

_____

_____

_____

What makes them interesting/valuable

_____

_____

_____

_____

_____

_____

Starting to take action

Choose one area from your list, and think about what you'd like to achieve. For instance, let's consider Sophie. Sophie had very bad relationships with her family, except for her sister, who was very important to her. Sophie chose relationships as an important area because she knew that she was happier around people. She thought about what kind of sister she would like to be, and said: 'I'd like to see Jess more often, and do what I can to protect her. She's still living at home and I could take her to the Citizens' Advice Bureau to see about moving out. And I'd like to contact my only remaining friend from school. I talk to her on Facebook but if I was feeling brave I could ask about meeting up!'

When you are planning actions, make the plan realistic, and think of goals that you might be able to achieve. For instance, Sophie decided that she would take her sister to the CAB, and that she'd message her friend. She didn't say, 'I'll sort my sister's housing out' or 'I'll go on a week's holiday with my friend.'

Think about who could help you with your goals – there are a lot of organisations that can help with voluntary work, for example, or with education.

In the box opposite, write down what you are going to do, and how you felt when you've done it. What might your next steps be?

My plans for action	How I felt when I'd done it	Next steps

A final word

We realise that everything that we've put in this book is very easy to write, and extremely hard to do. If you've been looking through it and thinking, 'They must be joking, they're lunatics,' then please don't dismiss us completely. Just try to make small changes in one or two areas. Don't write them off if they don't change everything all at once, but persevere. A journey of a thousand miles begins with a single step.

Good luck!

Appendix: Further reading and resources

Understanding emotions

The Compassionate Mind Foundation

Founded by Professor Paul Gilbert, this website has a number of books and resources that explain the origins of our emotion and thinking brains and how these lead to many common mental health problems.

www.compassionatemind.co.uk

Dialectical Behaviour Therapy

McKay, M., Wood, J. C., and Brantley, J. (2007). *The Dialectical Behavior Therapy Skills Workbook.* Oakland: New Harbinger Publications Inc.

Borderline Personality Disorder

Elliott, C. H. and Smith, L. L. (2009). *Borderline Personality Disorder for Dummies.* Indianapolis: Wiley Publishing Inc.

MIND

MIND is a mental health charity that offers a range of support services for people aged 18–64 who are experiencing mental health conditions that cause distress and impact adversely on the individual's life and well-being. MIND information on Borderline Personality Disorder:

www.mind.org.uk/information-support/types-of-mental-health-problems/personality-disorders

Self-harm and suicide

Campaign Against Living Miserably (CALM)

CALM provides a helpline for men who are struggling with suicidal thoughts. However, it is committed to offering help, support and information to anyone calling its service, regardless of age or gender. Its helpline and web chat service is available between 5 p.m. and midnight every day of the year.

☎ 0800 58 58 58

www.thecalmzone.net/get-help

www.thecalmzone.net

Calm Harm app

This is an app for your mobile. It is based on *Dialectical Behaviour Therapy* by Marsha Linehan, and uses many of the techniques found in this book. It is private and password protected.

www.stem4.org.uk/calmharm

The Samaritans

 116 123

www.samaritans.org

MIND

MIND's booklet on self-harm can be accessed via the following link:

www.mind.org.uk/information-support/types-of-mental-health-problems/self-harm

Recovery

Richmond Fellowship

Offers support for people recovering from mental health illness to find paid employment, voluntary work, education and training or to retain their current employment.

www.richmondfellowship.org.uk

Mindfulness

www.franticworld.com

www.bemindful.co.uk

www.headspace.com – this is an app for your mobile phone that supports you to develop the skills described in this book. You can download it for free, but be warned that if you want to develop your skills further there is a monthly subscription.

Relationships

Beck, Aaron T. (1988), *Love is Never Enough: How Couples Can Overcome Misunderstandings, Resolve Conflicts, and Solve Relationship Problems Through Cognitive Therapy*.

Epstein, Norma and Baucom, Donald (2002), *Enhanced Cognitive-Behavioural Therapy for Couples: A Contextual Approach*.

Brosan, Leonora and Todd, Gillian (2009), *Overcoming Stress*, Chapter 11 'Stress and Relationships'.

Relate

This is a national organisation which provides support for all aspects of relationship difficulties. Its website has a lot of helpful information as well as links to your nearest Relate and counsellors.

www.relate.org.uk